The Smart

30 Useful Engli

For Kids

By Rachel Mintz & David Levin
Palm Tree Publishing 2016

Dedicated to Eliya Oz Lavi Arad & Tomer

Copyright © 2016 Palm Tree Publishing

What are proverbs?
Proverbs are simple sayings that express a truth based on common sense or practical experience. They are popularly known and usually repeated until they become part of the spoken language. Proverbs contains wisdom, truth, morals, and traditional views in a memorizable form, and are handed down from generation to generation to express a truth based on common sense or experience.

List of Proverbs

1) A barking dog seldom bites.
2) A closed mouth catches no flies.
3) A bird in hand is worth two in a bush.
4) Better be the head of a dog than the tail of a lion.
5) Better lose the saddle than the horse.
6) Clothes don't make the man.
7) Don't count your chickens before they're hatched.
8) Don't judge a book by its cover.
9) Empty vessels make the most noise.
10) Every rose has its thorn.
11) Great oaks grow from small acorns.
12) Grief divided is made lighter.
13) Half a loaf is better than none
14) He who plays with fire gets burnt.
15) He laughs best who laughs last.
16) If you chase two rabbits, you will not catch either one.
17) In the land of the blind the one-eyed man is king.
18) It's no use crying over spilt milk.
19) A leopard cannot change its spots.
20) Little strokes fell good oaks.
21) Money doesn't grow on trees.
22) No pain, no gain.
23) No smoke without fire.
24) Once bitten, twice shy.
25) One man's trash is another man's treasure.
26) A picture is worth a thousand words.
27) Practice makes perfect.
28) Rome was not built in a day.
29) Stolen fruit is sweet / the sweetest
30) When the cat's away, the mice play.

1) A barking dog seldom bites.

Smart owl says: People who make big threats never usually carry them out. People who say they will do 'something bad' without meaning to do so in practice. Don't panic from every threat people say.

2) A closed mouth catches no flies.

Smart owl says: Don't talk too much if you don't won't get into trouble with what you say.

3) A bird in hand is
worth two in a bush.

Smart owl says: Don't be greedy running after things which seem better but are uncertain and stick with what you already have, even if it seems less.

4) Better be the head of a
dog than the tail of a lion.

Smart owl says: It is better to be the head or leader at the top of something (even if it is less prestigious) than a small or unimportant member of something big or fancy.

5) Better lose the saddle than the horse.

Smart owl says: Sometimes you may want to sacrifice something little, to avoid a much greater loss.

6) Clothes don't make the man.

Smart owl says: You should not judge a person solely by his appearance.

7) Don't count your chickens before they're hatched.

Smart owl says: You should not count on something before it really happens.

8) Don't judge a book by its cover.

Smart owl recommends: Don't judge the value of a thing simply by its appearance. Sometimes the outward appearance can be deceiving.

9) Empty vessels make the most noise.

The owl says: Those with the least talent and knowledge usually speak the most, speak the loudest, and create the most fuss.

The smart owl says: Always remember pretty much "nothing is perfect" and every good thing has some downside too.

11) Great oaks grow
from small acorns.

Smart owl knows: Great things may come from small beginnings. Plans that start off small or simple can become extremely large and successful.

12) Grief divided is made lighter.

The wise owl says: If you share your grief it becomes easier to bear.

13) Half a loaf is better than none.

The smart owl advise: You should be grateful for something, even if it is not as much as you wanted.

14) He who plays with fire gets burnt.

Smart owl says: If you behave in a risky way, you are likely to have problems.

15) He who laughs last, laughs best.

The owl says: If someone does something nasty to you, that person may feel satisfaction, but you will feel even more satisfaction when you get revenge in the end.

16) If you chase two rabbits,
you will not catch either one.

The wise owl says: If you try to do two things at the same time, you will not succeed in doing either of them. So focus only on one of them.

17) In the land of the blind
the one-eyed man is king.

The owl explains: Everything is relative. Even those with limited ability will be thought highly of by those with no ability at all.

18) It's no use crying over spilt milk.

Smart owl says: It is no use being angry or upset about something that has already happened which you cannot change.

19) The leopard cannot change its spots.

The owl says: It means a person's character, especially if it is bad, will not change, even if they pretend that it will. People's character doesn't change too easily.

20) Little strokes fell great oaks.

The smart owl knows: You can complete a large, intimidating task by steadily doing small parts of it. It's all about being persistent focusing on going forward even in small steps to achieve anything worthwhile.

21) Money doesn't grow on trees.

The wise owl says: You should be careful how much money you spend because there is only a limited amount of it. Money must be earned and is not easily acquired.

22) No pain, no gain.

The champion owl knows: The road to achievements run through hard work and success doesn't come without putting extra effort. Much can be accomplished by demanding practice and hard work.

23) No smoke without fire.

The owls says: A suspicion rumor usually has a basis in fact. There's usually some reason for a rumor.

24) Once bitten, twice shy.

The owl explains: Who has been hurt trying to do something will be far more careful the next time. Can be used to describe disappointment in relationships.

25) One man's trash is another man's treasure.

The owl says: People perceive things differently. Something that one person considers worthless may be considered valuable by someone else.

26) A picture is worth
a thousand words.

The owl's advice: An illustration, or picture can be more convincing or understandable by writing or saying. People believe what they see, not what they hear or read.

27) Practice makes perfect.

The smart owl knows: Doing something over and over makes you better at it. If you practice an activity enough, you will eventually master it.

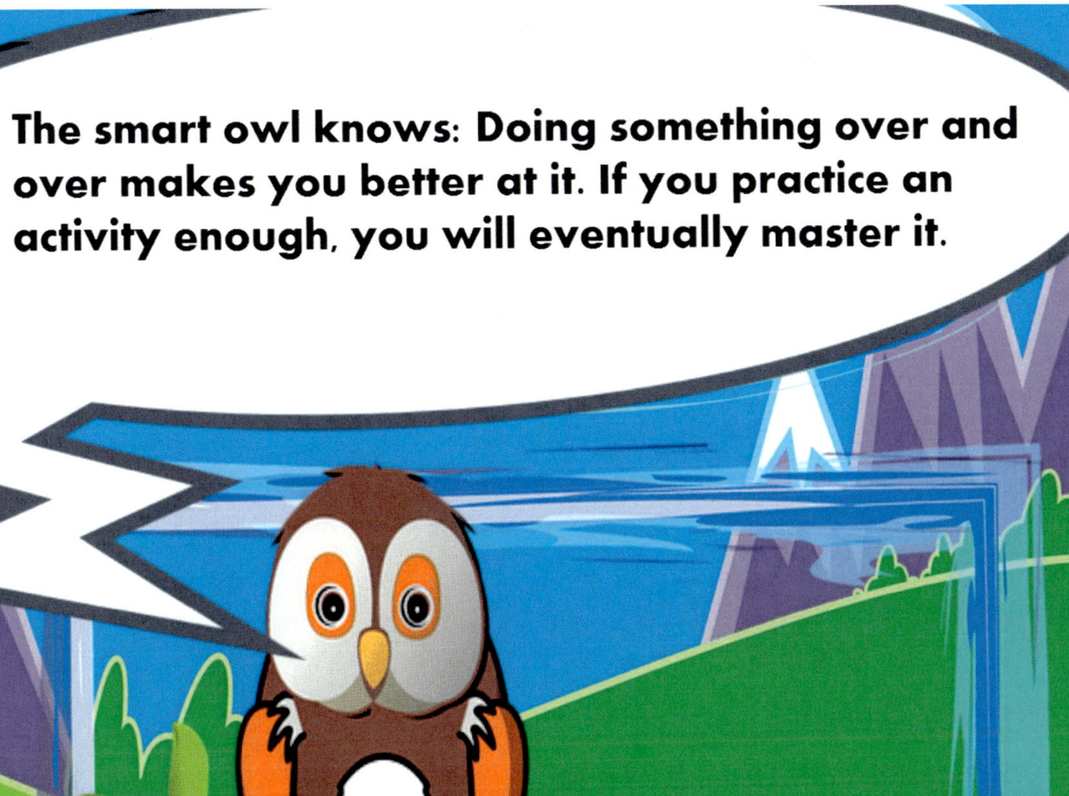

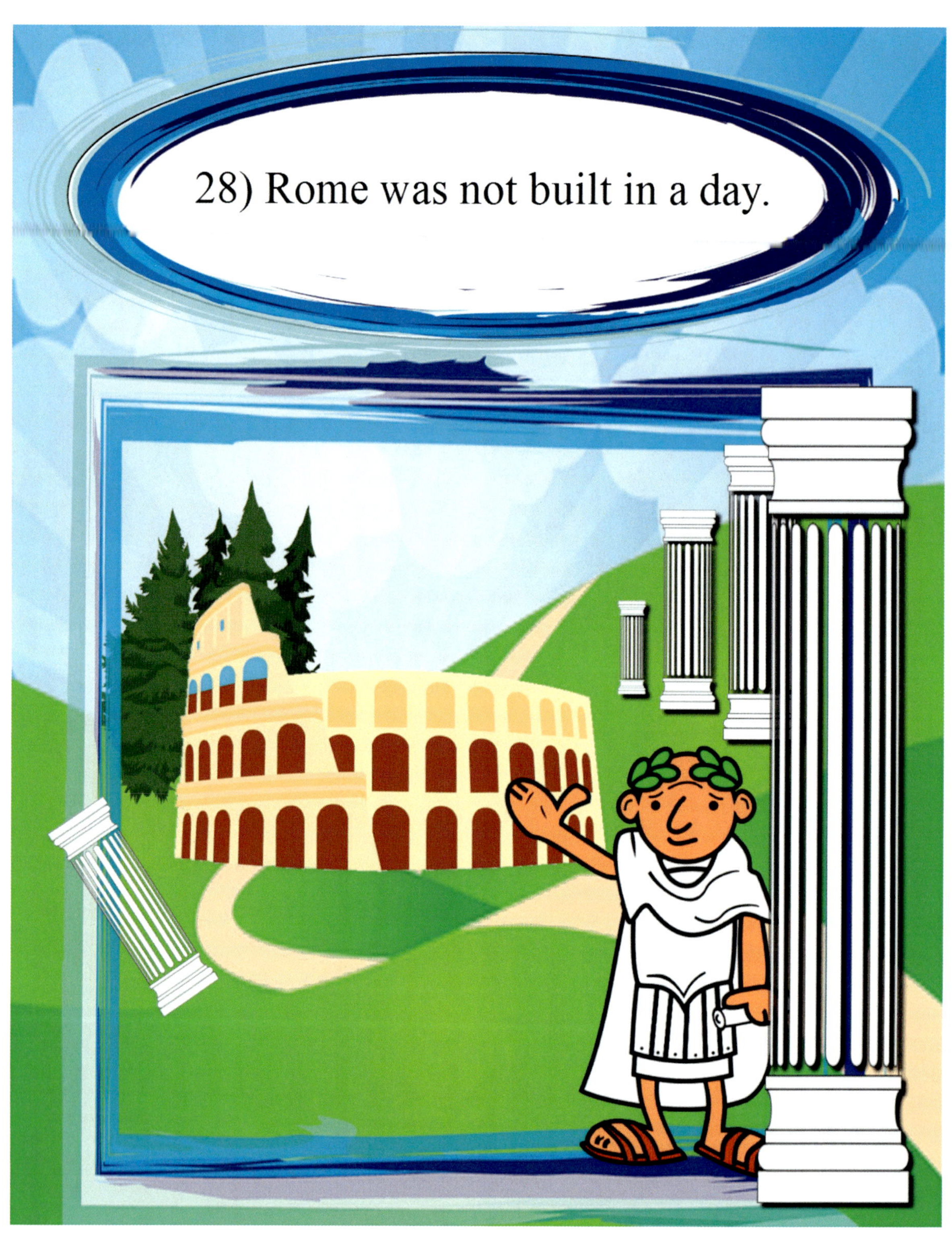

28) Rome was not built in a day.

The smart owl says: Great things require time and patience to be achieved. So keep investing efforts even if you do not see immediate results. It takes time to achieve something important.

29) Stolen fruit is the sweetest.

The smart owl warns: Getting things you aren't supposed to have, with the adrenaline and naughtiness acquiring them make them seem more fun.

30) When the cat's away, the mice play.

The wise owl knows: People take advantage of the absence of someone in authority to do as they like.

Proverbs Examples

1) A barking dog seldom bites.
   Jack said he would never be my friend if I touch his toys.. but mom said not to worry
   barking dog seldom bites.

2) A closed mouth catches no flies.
   The teacher heard July talking about sneaking from class and punished her. The teacher said
   a closed mouth catches no flies.

3) A bird in hand is worth two in a bush.
   John chose to get a day off this weekend, than to wait for the week vacation next year, he is
   right a bird in hand is worth two in a bush.

4) Better be the head of a dog than the tail of a lion.
   James is first of his class in math, while he got only 10th place in the school's team. He gets
   much more respect now from his classmates. The teacher said he better be the head of a dog
   than the tail of a lion.

5) Better lose the saddle than the horse.
   Jerry had a knee injury. His doctor said he had to chose whether to rest one game or play and
   risk the injury getting worse. If the knee got any worse he would not play again the whole
   season. His coach advised him to it's better to lose the saddle than the horse.

6) Clothes don't make the man.
   Sue's new friend wears loose pants and a rock star bandanna, everyone thinks he is a loser,
   yet he was accepted to Harvard law school. Sue kept saying the clothes don't make the man.

7) Don't count your chickens before they're hatched.
   Mary's dad thought he would sell his antique car for a fortune, so he took a big loan. But the
   car had an accident and he can't sell it now to anyone.. Her mom said he should have known
   not to count his chickens before they're hatched.

8) Don't judge a book by its cover.
   We went to a Hotel which looked very bad from outside. But the room was amazing and the
   service was wonderful. I guess you can't judge a book by its cover.

9) Empty vessels make the most noise.
   Peter was boasting he is a genius and smarter than any of us, yet he got last place in the IQ
   tests we did. Mom said the empty vessels makes the most noise.

10) Every rose has its thorn.
   The fancy restaurant we visited at my birthday had the most delicious dishes, but the waiter
   pants were dirty. My dad noted that every rose has its thorn.

11) Great oaks grow from small acorns.
   Last year we collected money for a friend's surgery. This year the city mayor said he will
   continue our efforts with an official fund for expensive surgeries. Great oaks grow from
   small acorns.

12) Grief divided is made lighter.
I was devastated when I have heard I did not manage to pass the auditions. I knew it was because the sound in the room was echoing. Then I heard it happened to many others that day and felt better. Oh well, said dad, grief divided is made lighter.

13) Half a loaf is better than none.
Dave wanted to be the first in his class both in chemistry and in physics. He wasn't too depressed when he found he was first only in physics, he knew half a loaf is better than none.

14) He who plays with fire gets burnt.
Eric had been involved in a car accident, but he had it coming as he was driving like a mad man. The police man told us he was not surprised the one who plays with fire will get burnt.

15) He laughs best who laughs last.
The kids made fun of Eliya because she was dancing funny. But apparently she was elected by the performance scout to lead the cheerleaders dance in the final game. Those who laughs best are those who laughs last.

16) If you chase two rabbits, you will not catch either one.
In the test Jenny tried to do as many math questions as she could, but doing math in a hasty way means most of them came out wrong. Her teacher said if you chase two rabbits, you will not catch either one, Jenny should have done less questions and solve them properly.

17) In the land of the blind the one-eyed man is king.
Jeremy who is in fifth grade and is very clumsy in basketball managed to score most of the points when he was playing with the second graders. The second grader's parents said in the land of the blind the one-eyed man is king.

18) It's no use crying over spilt milk.
Helen lost her camera last week in the school trip. She was still fussing about it a week later. The teacher told her to get over it, there is no use crying over spilt milk.

19) A leopard cannot change its spots.
Jack was caught last week stealing from the kid's lockers. He was caught doing it three years ago, and was warned not to do it again but a leopard cannot change its spots.

20) Little strokes fell good oaks.
Rob's dad has completed a book he was writing for two years. He wrote a few pages each week until the book was finished. The publisher said little strokes fell good oaks.

21) Money doesn't grow on trees.
Shelley has dropped her cellphone into the pool. It's the second time this happens to her. She asks her parents to buy her a brand new one, as if money doesn't grow on trees.

22) No pain, no gain.
Max flunked the tests for this year's tournament. He wasn't training so hard as he did last year. His parents were not surprised, no pain, no gain.

23) No smoke without fire.
The teachers could not prove who stole from the lockers, but they suspected it was Jack who was caught doing it a few times in the past. They said there's no smoke without fire.

24) Once bitten, twice shy.
Roy thought to offer Jill to go out with him, but since he was turned down by Rosie he lost all his confidence, his buddy said once bitten, twice shy.

25) One man's trash is another man's treasure.
We did a garage sale last week, and someone came and bought my old Sony Play Station. He was so happy about it, he never had a Play Station game before, one man's trash is another man's treasure.

26) A picture is worth a thousand words.
Becky tried to describe the new science project she has built. But the teacher didn't quite understand. Once Becky showed her teacher the diagram, the teacher was pleased she said a picture is worth a thousand words.

27) Practice makes perfect.
Ronny has been practicing so hard for a few weeks she was elected for the best ballet dancer in her class. She even did better than the teacher's daughter, no doubt practice makes perfect.

28) Rome was not built in a day.
Edgar was disappointed the new garden he worked on was not ready for the class visit. Mom told him not to worry, even Rome was not built in a day.

29) Stolen fruit is sweet / the sweetest
Jack was very pleased with the new shoes he managed to sneak from the locker. He thought they were better than the shoes he had, stolen fruit is the sweetest.

30) When the cat's away, the mice play.
The music teacher had to leave the lesson in the middle. Once he was gone the kids stopped practicing and began to play with their mobile phones. When headmaster showed up he said when the cat's away, the mice play.

Proverbs Quiz:

What do you say when...

1. Someone is not putting enough efforts and expects to succeed?
2. There is no proof about someone, but his is still a suspect of something?
3. Someone is not too accountable to the money they spend?
4. Small actions add up to a great change?
5. When someone keeps behaving badly over and over again?
6. When the best way to explain something is not by words?
7. When it is better to be grateful to a smaller success than to no success at all?
8. Someone is not focusing on one issue but is going after too many goals?
9. Someone is getting himself in to trouble by speaking at the wrong time or place?
10. When people do not stay self disciplined unless they are watched over by someone else?

See answers upside down:

1. No pain, no gain.
2. There is no smoke without fire.
3. Money doesn't grow on trees.
4. Little strokes fell good oaks.
5. A leopard cannot change its spots.
6. A picture is worth a thousand words.
7. Half a loaf is better than none.
8. If you chase two rabbits, you will not catch either one.
9. A closed mouth catches no flies.
10. When the cat's away, the mice play.

The Smart Owl's
30 Useful English Proverbs For Kids

The End

If you have found a typo error, or want to ask a question
about a proverb or maybe you have enjoyed this book and
want to share your review ;-) with other parents.
Please do so at the review page on Amazon.
We read and answer every comment.

More from the 'Fun Books For Children' series.

Fun Book For Passover – A 60+ pages of puzzles and games for kids, to help them remember the main themes of the Passover Story.
What is the Seder, Haggadah, Afikoman, The Ten Plagues, What is Chametz, What is Matzah, Passover Songs.

Rosh Ha Shanah Fun Book – With this book the kids learn about the the Jewish New Year. The main traditions, what is Shofar, what do we bless upon, and the common rituals of this festival.

Children Learn About Yom Kippur – The sacred day on the Jewish calendar. Why do we fast, what rituals are common. What is Kol Nidrei, what is the ritual of Kaparot, what do we bless one another during this day?

Sukkot Fun Book – One of the Three Pilgrimage festivals on the Jewish calendar. What are the Four Spices (Arba Minim), what is Sukkah? What are the main traditions of Sukkot?

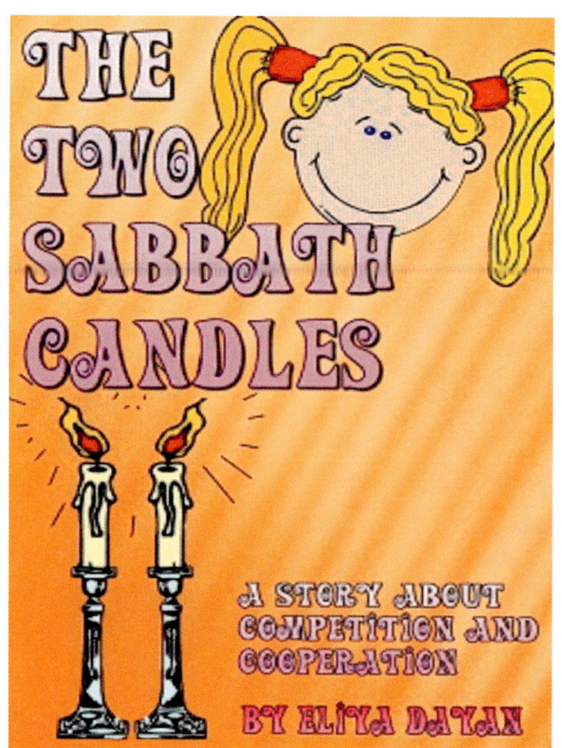

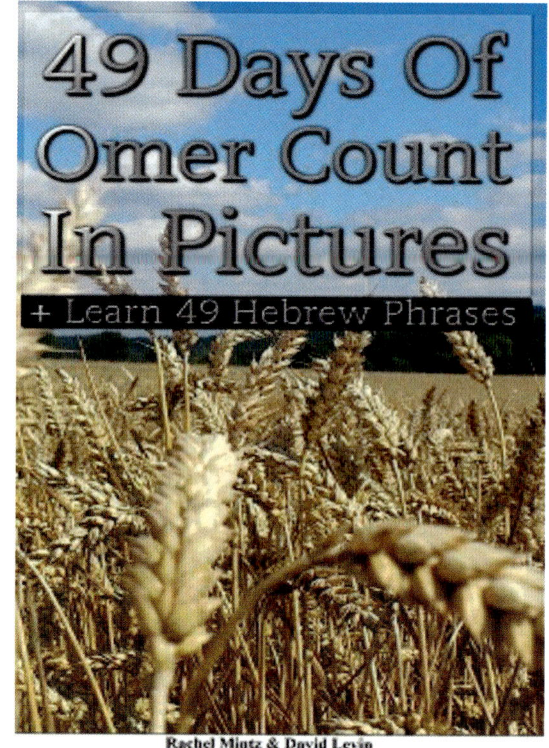

Two Sabbath Candles – Is a story written by a 10 years old author, it's about family, brother sister competition and cooperation. With the Sabbath Candles teaching the kid a wise lesson.

49 Days of Omer Counting in Pictures – Is a photo album of 49 beautiful images of earth's nature scenery. In each of the 49 images there is the daily **Omer Counting** blessing in Hebrew and English + One simple Hebrew (translated) phrase to learn.

You have finished reading

The Smart Owl's
30 Useful English Proverbs For Kids

Please leave a REVIEW to help parents who consider buying this book.

Manufactured by Amazon.ca
Bolton, ON